Hey kids! The flag at the top of these pages will appear to wave as you flip through the pages really fast!

The Here & Now Reproducible Book of

The DAY That Was DIFFERENT™

September 11, 2001
When Terrorists Attacked America

by
award-winning children's author
Carole Marsh

For additional information, go to our website at **www.gallopade.com**.

The Here & Now™ Team

Carole Marsh	Michael Longmeyer
Cecil Anderson	Diana Sullivan
Victoria DeJoy	Chad Beard
Jeff West	Billie Walburn
Kathy Zimmer	Terry Briggs
Sherry Moss	Bob Longmeyer
Steven Saint-Laurent	
Michele Yother	

Published by

GALLOPADE™ INTERNATIONAL

800-536-2GET
www.gallopade.com

Gallopade is proud to be a member of these educational organizations and associations:

2

The DAY That Was DIFFERENT™

The Day That Was Different: September 11, 2001—
When America Was Attacked by Terrorists

The Day That Was Different: September 11, 2001—
When America Was Attacked by Terrorists (Activity Pack)

United We Stand!: America's War Against Terrorism

United We Stand!: America's War Against Terrorism (Activity Pack)

PATRIOTIC FAVORITES™

America the Beautiful! Illustrated Lyrics
for Kids to Color, Say, and Display

The Pledge of Allegiance. . .to Color, Say, and Display

My American Flag!: Flag, Facts, and How to Display Properly

Patriotic Favorites Coloring and Activity Book

The Young Patriot's Book of Puzzles, Games, Riddles,
Stories, Poems, and Activities

George W. Bush: America's Newest President,
and His White House Family!

3

Table of Contents

A Word From The Author

Dear Students,

When I was first learning to write mystery books for boys and girls, I was reminded to quickly get to the "day that was different!" You know: the day the ghost was first seen, the day the work of art disappeared, the day the "thing" happened that really got the mystery underway!

For many years, I have been writing about days that were different in history: the day all those guys signed that piece of paper called the Declaration of Independence; the day the Japanese bombed Pearl Harbor in Hawaii; the day men first stood on the Moon!

On September 11, 2001, we all—young and old, alike—witnessed a day that was certainly different. It was an ordinary school and work day for most of us . . . at least until the time that sunny morning when airplanes hijacked by terrorists began to be used as missiles in an attack on America.

Some "different" days are good: the first day we ever go to school; our 16th birthday; the first time we get to vote. Some "different" days are bad, and September 11 was one of the worst days for most of us in our entire lifetime so far.

In a mystery book, when the day that is different comes, everyone is always surprised, shocked, stunned, but soon gets to work solving the mystery. On September 11, all Americans were surprised, shocked, and stunned—but soon got busy helping, thinking, planning, and learning. We wanted to know what had happened, and why. How we could help. What would happen next? How could we put a stop to such terrible terrorist actions in the future?

The most important thing about the very different day of September 11, 2001 may be how we respond, what we learn, and how we act and react from now on. I hope this book helps.

Carole Marsh
Peachtree City, Georgia USA

P.S.: As events continue to unfold, please check our Gallopade website for updates and additional information.

What Happened on September 11, 2001, and What it Means

For most of us, Tuesday, September 11, 2001 was an ordinary school or work day. You may have been in class at your desk. You may have been talking to a friend or teacher. No matter where you were or what you were doing, at some time you probably heard that something bad had happened.

What Happened?

That morning, terrorists hijacked four airplanes. In a short time, these terrorists flew one plane into an office building of the World Trade Center in New York City. Soon after, another airplane hit a second World Trade Center building. Some people were able to escape from the buildings before both of them collapsed. Many people were not able to escape in time.

In the meantime, terrorists flew an airplane into the Pentagon building in our nation's capital, Washington, D.C. This building is very large and only part of it was hit. Some people escaped; some did not. Shortly after this, the last plane crashed in a field in the state of Pennsylvania. It is believed that the terrorists may have planned to crash this plane into the White House or some other target, but that passengers on board prevented this from happening.

Very soon, most of us realized that America was under attack. It appeared that the attack was over. We knew that all the people on all four airplanes had died. It was clear that probably thousands of people had died in the office buildings. However, rescuers were trying to save anyone who had survived. And everyone in America was wondering why this had happened, what it meant, and what would happen next. We were afraid and we were sad.

This is where I was when I heard the news: _____

This is what I felt when I heard the news: _____

_____

_____

_____

terrorist: a person who does bad things, usually with no warning, and often against innocent people

hijack: the illegal overtaking of an airplane

Check which things you think this terrible event means:

○ America has a problem to solve
○ Many people's lives have been changed
○ Everyone will be sad for a long time
○ Everyone will be angry and want to do something
○ America will never recover from this attack
○ Things will never be back to normal

If you checked the first four, you are right; if you did not check the last two you are right. A tragedy like this always means change, but it does not mean that things will not be "ok" in the future.

AS WE LEARNED MORE . . .

It is not surprising that as soon as we learned what had happened (after all, the events appeared live on the morning television news shows!), we were glued to reporters' every word. However, the news was not coming from the reporters, it was coming from people at the scene of the disaster . . . people on cell phones . . . and, slowly, from government and airline officials.

"I couldn't believe what I saw! I was home drinking coffee and watching tv, and this airplane just crashed right into the World Trade Center. I thought it was a small plane, an accident. And then in just a few minutes another airplane—a big one!—crashed into another World Trade Center tower. I gasped! I just couldn't believe it! Then in a minute, they said an airplane had crashed into the Pentagon. And, that one was flying around Pennsylvania with hijackers on board. When I began to hear of all the people who had died, I cried."—A mother

Most students were in school, unable to follow the unfolding story, except on radio or as teachers shared new information. It was later widely reported how well schools and students had handled the situation, which parents greatly appreciated. While parents and teachers tried to protect younger students from the news, older students wanted to know what was going on, if they were safe, and what would happen next.

"Everyone at school was calm on the outside, but inside we were scared and sad. It was hard to believe! Our teachers took good care of us. Some parents came to get their kids. The bad news was bad, but I was glad to see how we all stuck together during this really scary morning."—a student

As the day went on, and we learned more facts, we knew it was a terrible tragedy, but we were relieved to see so many people who were safe, who were helping, and who were telling us the attacks were over.

CHECK WHERE YOU GOT MOST OF YOUR FACTS:

☐ Television ☐ Radio ☐ Newspaper ☐ Mom ☐ Dad

☐ Teacher ☐ Principal ☐ Friends ☐ Internet

7

SEPTEMBER 11, 2001: A TIMELINE OF SIGNIFICANT EVENTS

History is what happens. It is the facts, not rumor or guesses. Sometimes, we know exactly what happened and when. But often, it takes time for all the facts to come out. As time goes by, we have more time to analyze and think about what happened. This time period gives us a clearer and more accurate understanding of events. If we are smart, we can learn from history. Here is a timeline for you to complete in the days and weeks ahead.

When	What Happened
Sept. 11	• Four airplanes hijacked; 2 crash into World Trade Center buildings in New York City; 1 crashes into Pentagon in Washington, D.C.; 1 crashes in rural Pennsylvania; some people escape or are rescued; many die from the explosion or when the WTC buildings collapse • President Bush returns to the capital and speaks to Americans on TV
Sept. 12–14	• Rescuers continue to search for survivors; airports are shut down; FBI and others try to learn who the terrorists are; President Bush assures us we are safe and that we will find and punish the attackers
Sept. 14	• National day of prayer; people pray and attend religious services; many Americans display flags and hold candlelight vigils • President Bush works with world leaders on capturing the terrorists; most nations around the world support America
Mid to Late September	• Hijackers identified • FBI searches for other possible terrorists • Refugees flee Afghanistan •America and other nations donate food and other supplies to Afghan refugees • U.S. military goes on heightened alert and some troops are deployed
October	• NATO declares that the attack on America was an attack on <u>all</u> North Atlantic Treaty Organization nations • On October 7, U.S. and other military forces made the first attacks on targets throughout Afghanistan
2001 - ?	• America commits to a war against terrorism

8

AFTER SEPTEMBER 11, 2001: A TIMELINE OF SIGNIFICANT EVENTS

Now, you pick up the story as events unfold:

When	What Happened

Other notes: _____

_____

_____

_____

THE GEOGRAPHY OF TERRORISM:
WHAT PLACES WERE INVOLVED ON SEPTEMBER 11, 2001?

Geography matters; that's why we study it in school! No matter where you live and go to school, on the day the terrorists attacked America, you probably wondered *Where is that? How close? Am I in danger? Is anyone I know involved?*

Several main geographic places are related to the day that terrorists hijacked four airplanes and used them to attack the World Trade Center and the Pentagon, and one plane crashed before hitting a target:

In the United States	Outside of the United States
•New York City	•Afghanistan
• Boston, Massachusetts	•Pakistan
•Washington, D.C.	•the Middle East
•Newark, New Jersey	
•Shanksville, Pennsylvania	

Sometimes we refer to the place where a disastrous event takes place as "ground zero." Our reaction may vary depending on how close we are to "ground zero." If we are close, we may be involved in the crisis; we may be able to help. If we are far away, we may feel safe, but we may wish we could be closer to help. Circle the "ground zero" locations on the map here.

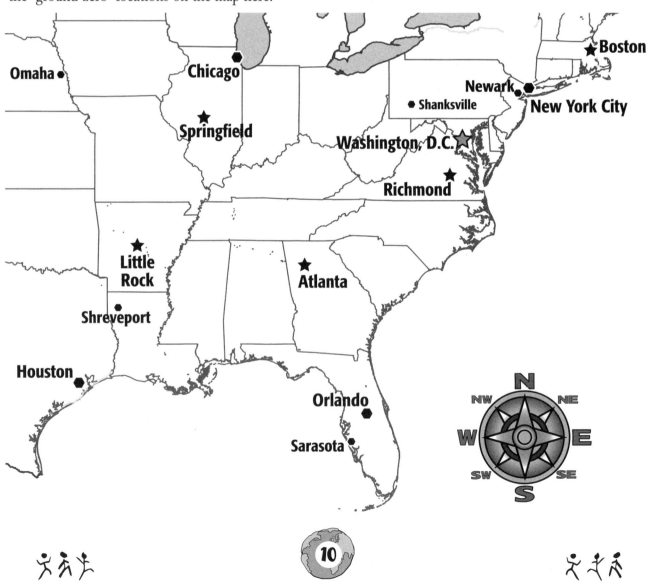

THE GEOGRAPHY OF TERRORISM:
A STUDENT'S MAP OF AFGHANISTAN

It is believed that the terrorists who planned the hijackings and attacks on America are from the country of Afghanistan. These terrorists have ties with the nation of Pakistan. In addition, Afghanistan has ethnic and religious ties with the Middle East. The Middle East has long been one area where terrorists are active. Answer the following questions:

1. Afghanistan is…

_____ close to _____ far away from…the United States.

2. By looking at the map below, you can tell that Afghanistan and Pakistan are geographic

_____ _____ _____ _____ _____ _____ _____ _____ _____.

Afghanistan and America are not very similar. America is made up of a collection of 50 states with many cities and many citizens. Afghanistan is a sparsely populated country with a rugged terrain of mountains and caves.

Check which you think each country has:	America	Afghanistan
A capital city	_____	_____
Geographic borders	_____	_____
Many large cities	_____	_____
Many millions of citizens	_____	_____

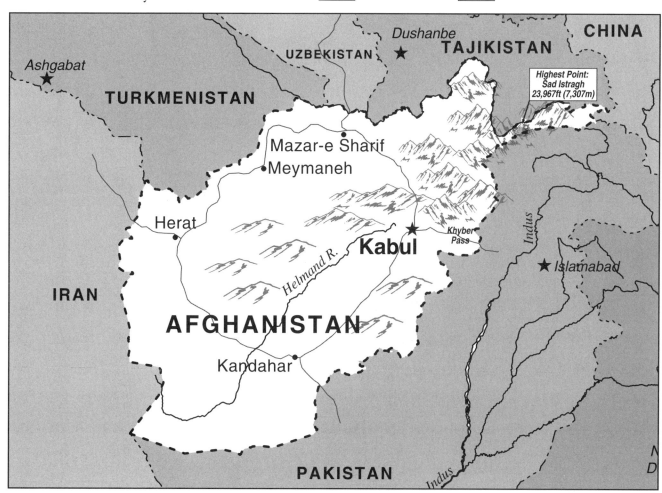

Answers: 1. Far away from…Afghanistan is at least 6,750 miles from the U.S. 2. neighbors

©Carole Marsh/Gallopade International/800-536-2GET/www.gallopade.com/Here & Now Series–The Day That Was Different

What is the World Trade Center?

The World Trade Center is a group of buildings located on the lower end of the island of Manhattan in New York City. The WTC includes office towers, hotels, restaurants, shops, and many other types of establishments. The World Trade Center has long been recognized as a main focal point of international business activity. It is near Wall Street where the New York Stock Exchange is located. The World Trade Center's twin towers were each more than 100 stories tall. High-speed elevators would take workers to their offices and visitors to an observation deck, where they could see for many miles all around New York City. These tall buildings were also part of New York City's beautiful skyline. You often see them pictured on post cards.

The World Trade Center was considered an architectural and engineering marvel. The buildings were constructed to withstand hurricanes and earthquakes. They were built of strong steel. But the enemy of steel is very high heat. Terrorists crashed two airplanes into these buildings on September 11, 2001. The planes were filled with large amounts of fuel. This fuel created fires so hot that they melted the steel which caused the buildings to collapse. Other buildings were damaged, too. Some may have to be taken down. It will take a long time to clean up this area.

12

The World Trade Center of the Future

One day, something new will be built where the twin office towers of the World Trade Center once stood. Some people think the towers should be rebuilt. Others think a park or other memorial would be appropriate. Draw what you would like to see built there in the box below.

13

WHAT IS THE PENTAGON? WHY DID THE TERRORISTS PICK ON THAT BUILDING?

The Pentagon is a very amazing building! It looks like this: ⟹

As you can see, a "pentagon" has _____ sides. The Pentagon is the building where the people who run America's military work. Why did the terrorists choose to fly a hijacked airplane into the Pentagon building? We do not know. It may be that they really intended to attack the White House or another building, but failed. They may have flown into the Pentagon because it is such an important part of U.S. military operations. Perhaps they thought it would hurt our military or even stop our military from operating. Of course, this is not true!

Some people escaped from the part of the Pentagon that was attacked. Others did not. All aboard the aircraft were killed. Only a small part of the building was actually destroyed. It will take a long time and cost a lot of money, but the Pentagon will be rebuilt. In the meantime, the Pentagon is "back in business" with military personnel hard at work to see that such an attack never happens again.

The Pentagon is just one of the many buildings located in our nation's capital, Washington, D.C. Some other structures include:

- White House _____
- Capitol _____
- Supreme Court _____
- Washington Monument _____
- Jefferson Memorial _____
- Lincoln Memorial _____

Match the landmarks above with the illustrations shown!

Now, answer the following questions:

Have you ever visited Washington, D.C.?: ___YES ___NO

Would you like to visit our nation's capital?: ___YES ___NO

List places you would like to visit while you are there:

_____ _____

_____ _____

_____ _____

Answers: A "pentagon" has 5 sides. White House–E; Capitol–F; Supreme Court–D; Washington Monument–B; Jefferson Memorial–C; Lincoln Memorial–A

14

Camp David: A Place to Talk Peace

One place we read about during and after the September 11, 2001 terrorist attacks was Camp David. Camp David is a 134-acre (54.23- hectare) retreat for the President, his family, and guests. It is located in the 10,000-acre (4,047-hectare) Catoctin Mountain Park, near Thurmont, Maryland.

On the morning of September 11, officials learned that an airplane had been hijacked and turned around in Ohio and headed back toward the Washington, D.C. area. The plane crashed in Pennsylvania. Some people feared that the hijackers had plans to crash the plane into the White House, or another target, such as Camp David.

CAMP DAVID

Trivia!

When Franklin D. Roosevelt was president, he spent weekends aboard the presidential yacht, the Potomac, or in Hyde Park, New York. During World War II, the Secret Service worried about the president's safety while he was on the yacht. So, they looked for a cool place in the mountains near Washington, D.C. Camp Hi Catoctin was chosen after President Roosevelt visited it in April 1942.

Many historical events have taken place at Camp David—the planning of the Normandy invasion during World War II; discussions of the Bay of Pigs situation with Cuba in 1961; the Camp David Peace Accords between Israel and Egypt in 1979; and many discussions with foreign dignitaries and world leaders.

The government bought the land, which had rough terrain and eroded soil, in 1936 with plans to turn the area back into productive land. The New Deal's Works Progress Administration (WPA) and the Civilian Conservation Corps (CCC) worked together to create the Catoctin Recreational Demonstration Area in 1939. Camp Misty Mount was built and first used by the Maryland League for Crippled Children. However, the area around Camp Misty Mount was too hard to negotiate in a wheelchair, so a second camp was built, Camp Greentop. During the winter of 1938-39, Camp Hi Catoctin, a third camp, was built for use as a family camp for federal employees.

Trivia!

President Eisenhower had a bomb shelter built at Camp David which is located 65 feet (19.8 meters) underground!

President Roosevelt renamed the camp "Shangri-La" from James Hilton's novel Lost Horizon. Harry Truman called the retreat the summer White House. In 1953, Dwight D. Eisenhower renamed it Camp David to honor his grandson, David.

The main lodge at Camp David was made by connecting four cabins and is named Aspen. Now, Camp David is ready for President George W. Bush and his family to use and enjoy!

15

The Religion of Islam and

There are many religions in the world. One of the major world religions is Islam. The people who practice the Islamic faith are called Muslims. The center of Islam is Mecca, in Saudi Arabia.

Islam is a very old religion. Its practitioners believe in God, whom they call Allah, and peace. Sometimes we hear the term "fundamentalists." In Islam this means Muslims who follow certain good rules: they do not believe in killing, stealing, drinking alcohol, gambling, and other such things.

Islam Fast Facts:

- **Islam:** Arabic for "submission," "surrender," or "commitment"
- **Mohammed:** prophet who started Islam
- **Allah:** what Muslims call God
- **Muslims:** followers of Islam
- **Some places where Islam is practiced:** Pakistan, India, Indonesia, China, United States
- **Mecca:** Islam's holy city
- **Qu'ran (Koran):** Sacred book of the Muslims
- **Mosque:** Muslim place of worship
- **Ramadan:** Muslim holy month
- Muslims pray five times each day
- Most Muslims are not Arabs

It is believed that the terrorists who attacked New York City and Washington, D.C. on September 11, 2001 were Islamic. Does this mean that Muslims are bad people and Islam is a bad religion? No, of course not.

Most Muslims are very good and peaceful people, like those of other religions. Any religion can have a very few people who are *fanatics*. They take good ideas and twist them until they become bad ideas. Why? Because these bad ideas help them achieve their own personal goals, not the goals of the whole group of believers.

16

the Muslims Who Practice It

We may look at a person and not know their religion. However, we often see Muslims dressed in long dresses (women) or wearing turbans and long beards (men). This is one way they express their religion. They may look different, but that is not what makes them bad or good.

fanatic: a person who thinks very differently from most people and may use their beliefs to justify acts of hatred

There are many Muslims in America. Some were killed when fanatic Islamic terrorists attacked America on September 11, 2001. The terrorists insisted they were fighting a "holy war" (*jihad*) because their religion required it.

But most Muslims disagree. They know that Islam is about peace, not war. They are good citizens and are just as sad as everyone else over these attacks. Perhaps they are even sadder because they know that someone of their religion committed these terrible deeds. Their religion does not believe in doing such bad things. However, some people who practice Islam (and other religions) become *fanatics*. They develop different beliefs and often convince themselves that these beliefs mean they can (and even should) do bad things for what they think is a good reason. Most people of any religion (or even with no religious beliefs) think they are very, very wrong!

Throughout history, it has not been uncommon for people to do bad things in the name of religion. Usually this is just an excuse to get their way or to justify doing something bad to achieve their own goals. Of course, sometimes such fanatics believe they are doing the right thing, which only makes them more determined and more dangerous.

Fill-in-the-blanks:

Islam is a religion of ___ ___ ___ ___ ___. If I believe in Islam, I am called a ___ ___ ___ ___ ___ ___. In the Islamic religion, we call God ___ ___ ___ ___ ___. I __may/__may not dress differently than other kids. I feel ___ ___ ___ that a few people of my religion committed terrorist acts. I __do/__do not believe in terrorists' idea of a "holy war."

Answer: peace; Muslim; Allah; may or may not; bad or sad or mad; Which did you choose?

17

What is Terrorism? Why Does it Exist? Is it New in History?

The attacks on America on September 11, 2001 brought all kinds of questions to our minds. We may have heard of terrorists and terrorism before. We may know that even an American can be a terrorist or perform a terroristic act, such as the bombing of a government building in Oklahoma City, Oklahoma on April 19, 1995. However, we usually think of terrorism as car bombs and other activities that happen in other countries. On this day, we found out that, unfortunately, this is not the case.

The United States has experienced another major other attack of terrorism on our own soil by non-Americans. This was the surprise attack on Pearl Harbor in Hawaii on December 7, 1941. This was an attack by the Japanese air force on an American naval base. More than 2,500 people were killed, most of them American military workers. This attack caused America to declare war on Japan and to join in World War II, which America and its allies eventually won.

The far more recent attack on America by outsiders was quite different. The primary place attacked was a city, not a military complex. The people who died were civilians, not soldiers. The attackers were not soldiers, either, but religious fanatics. It is not surprising that most of the world joined with America to express that terrorism is *always* wrong. Moreover, America and other democratic countries know that peace is better than war, and that diplomacy is better than fighting. These nations are determined to join together to put an end to terrorism.

One thing terrorists have in common is that they are cowards. They hide so that they cannot be found. They are unwilling to discuss problems. And, they are not respected by anyone except their fellow terrorists.

Check the items that you believe diplomacy can work out:

- [ ] Disagreements about geographic borders
- [ ] Disagreements over religious freedoms
- [ ] Abuses of the rights of citizens
- [ ] Arguments within a nation
- [ ] Arguments among nations

fanatic: a person who thinks very differently from most people and may use their beliefs to justify acts of hatred

diplomacy: using meetings, talking, and discussion to work out disagreements

18

WHAT'S NEXT IN TERRORISM?

Many people fear that one day, terrorists might use bio-warfare to attack nations. This is the use of chemicals or germs as weapons of war. Terrorists are always thinking of new ways to terrorize people. No wonder that following the September 11, 2001 attack on America by terrorists, most of the world's nations agreed to join in a war to end such terrorism!

Once, terrorists used weapons such as guns and bombs to achieve their goals. Today, they also use computers to transfer funds to spend on terrorism, and cell phones to communicate with one another. Some terrorists (although very few and on a limited basis) have used chemicals or germs.

In a subway in Japan, terrorists released a poisonous chemical gas which made many people very sick. Even in American history, we know that sometimes blankets infected with the disease smallpox were given as "gifts" (Gee, thanks?) to Native Americans. Since they had no immunity to the "white man's" diseases, many were infected and died.

Today, many people worry about the use of chemicals or germs to terrorize people and create worry and fear. There are many precautions we can take against such "bio-warfare":
- Keep our public health systems strong
- Enforce tight security of our water systems
- Stockpile antidotes to some diseases, which we are not today immunized against

Most nations of the world are very opposed to any type of war based on chemicals or germs. Agreements have been put into place to destroy such materials. During the war on terrorism, everyone will be working to make sure terrorists cannot create or otherwise get their hands on such weapons.

DID YOU KNOW?:

In the 1960s, American kids often feared that we would have a nuclear war. Some people were so afraid of this that they built "bomb shelters" filled with food, water, bedding, lanterns, and other supplies in case of a nuclear attack. Schools even had "drills" of what to do in case of an attack. Today, even though more nations have the capability to make a nuclear bomb, it is believed that such a threat is very remote. PS: Most folks did away with their "bomb shelters" long ago!

19

The Government in Charge: What Happens When America Suffers an Attack?

Every nation tries to be prepared for all types of disasters and catastrophes. This may be a weather disaster such as a hurricane. It may be an economic crisis such as the 1929 collapse of the American stock market. It may be an internal problem, such as the U.S. Civil War. Or it may be an act of war by another nation. Sometimes, as we saw on September 11, 2001, it can be an act of terrorism.

The main way that the United States prepares for such a disaster is prevention. You can't prevent a hurricane (so far!), but if you have advance information, you can often stop a terrorist act before it happens. Sometimes, advance warnings can come from "intelligence"— information the military works to uncover. Other times, terrorists brag ahead of time about what they plan to do.

When an attack does take place, we can at least be reassured that our government already has plans for how to handle most types of situations. Here are just a few of the helpful things that occur:

- The president is moved to a safe location, as are other government and military leaders

- Actions are taken first to help those in need and then to assure that no other attacks take place, if at all possible

- Even while recovery is underway, the nation's leaders work on how to respond to the situation and how to prevent future such disasters

Circle ways you saw America respond to the recent attacks:

TRAINED RESCUERS SENT TO THE SCENE

AIRPLANE TRAFFIC STOPPED   AIRPORTS CLOSED

PRESIDENT SPOKE TO NATION MANY TIMES

BLOOD COLLECTED FOR TRANSFUSIONS

MILITARY PERSONNEL CALLED TO SERVICE

OTHER: _____

_____

_____

20

SAFETY & SECURITY

Top Priorities When Presidents Travel!

While George W. Bush was still living in Texas, he probably liked to take a pick-up truck out for a ride around his ranch. But today, when President George W. Bush wants to travel, he has a choice of limousine, helicopter, or a Boeing 747-200B aircraft.

The Secret Service won't say how many presidential limousines there are, but they are all designed to protect the president's life, wherever he goes.

The White House fleet includes three 1993 black Cadillac parade limousines. The limousines were built by General Motors for an estimated cost of $10 million. They are leased to the president for $1 a year.

Instead of a television and a refrigerator, you will find telephone and radio equipment inside the presidential limousines. A power glass window with a privacy shade separates the driver from the president. The right rear door has a special locking system that stops it from being opened too quickly. Blast shields are built into the floor to protect the limousines from grenades. The limousines also have 11-inch running boards on them for Secret Service agents to stand on.

The presidential limousines don't have guns mounted on them, but the Secret Service agents are all armed. The limousines are usually followed by Chevrolet Suburbans whose passengers are Secret Service agents who carry automatic weapons.

The mission of the Executive Flight Detachment of Marine Helicopter Squadron One (HMX-1) at Quantico, Virginia is transporting the president wherever business takes him. The squadron has four different helicopters used to fly the president. When the president flies in one of these, it is called "Marine One."

Before any planned presidential flight, the crew members have a rehearsal flight to the site to make sure "Marine One" is mechanically sound. The rehearsal flight gives crew members time to fix any problems before the president gets aboard the helicopter.

When the president is aboard one of the two Boeing 747s which provide air transport for the president, that plane is referred to as "Air Force One." The 89th Military Airlift Wing at Andrews Air Force Base in Maryland is responsible for Air Force One.

The flying "Oval Office" in Air Force One includes a conference/dining room, quarters for the president and first lady, and an office area for senior staff members. Two galleys (kitchens) can provide up to 100 meals at a time. It can carry up to 102 people, including 26 crew members.

On September 11, 2001, President Bush was in Florida speaking to school students. He was notified of the terrorist attacks and immediately left on Air Force One. To be sure he was safe, the president was flown to a secure location in Omaha, Nebraska. Then, accompanied by fighter jets on each side, Air Force One flew the president to Washington, D.C., where he went back to work in the White House.

©Carole Marsh/Gallopade International/800-536-2GET/www.gallopade.com/Here & Now Series–The Day That Was Different

Land of the Free: How a Democratic Country is Different

Some people say that one reason America was vulnerable to a terrorist attack like the one on September 11, 2001 is that we are a *democracy*. As a democratic country, we enjoy many freedoms:

- Citizens are allowed travel freely in and out of the country as well as across the states
- Immigrants are allowed to move to America
- Visitors to the United States are allowed to travel freely around the nation

One of the things we like best about our democratic nation is the freedom that it allows us. In spite of our freedom, we also have laws that people must obey while in our country, whether they are citizens or visitors. When people obey these laws, it helps protect our democratic way of life.

Not all nations are democracies. Their citizens may have many more rules and regulations. They may have laws that interfere with rights that are so ordinary to us that we may even take them for granted sometimes. In a non-democratic country, some people are leaders; others must follow these leaders . . . or else. Life is very different from ours under these circumstances.

Some people may be jealous of our democratic nation. They may not understand it. They may feel threatened by the power of a country where free will rules. They may even take advantage of our open way of life to harm us. It appears that some of the terrorists who attacked New York and Washington, D.C. had been living in America, perhaps even for years. But they were not working hard like most citizens; they were up to no good, plotting and planning their attacks.

democracy: a country where the people rule

Circle the good things about living in a democracy:

RIGHT TO ELECT OWN LEADERS   FREEDOM OF SPEECH

RIGHT TO BEAR ARMS   FREEDOM TO LIVE ANYWHERE

RIGHT TO OWN PROPERTY   RIGHT TO BE EDUCATED

FREE TO TRAVEL AT WILL

ADD YOUR IDEAS:

_____

_____

_____

Democracy Makes a Difference!

You could say that there are two types of nations in the world: democratic and non-democratic. It's sort of like a club, and almost everyone would agree that belonging to the "democratic" club is best!

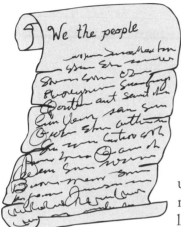

Although democracies can be different, they have one thing in common: THE PEOPLE ARE IN CHARGE. In America, we know that we elect our leaders to represent us. That's what a democracy is: "of the people, by the people, for the people."

If you live in a democracy, you understand how wonderful it is. In fact, it might be hard for us to even imagine living in a place where we cannot speak freely, travel at will, vote, run for office, be entitled to a speedy trial, and other "freedoms" and "rights."

Some people who do not live in a democratic nation wish they did. Perhaps, once, their nation was a democracy. If a few people took over the country, against the will of the majority, this democracy may have gone by the wayside.

Some people who do not live in a democracy do not understand it. Perhaps all they have ever known is being "ruled" like they were children. Or, they may be jealous of America and other democratic countries. Instead of working to build a democracy, they may react by trying to tear down other democracies.

We know how America got to be a democracy: we went to war and fought England for our freedom. We have fought many times to protect our democratic way of life. We are not likely to give up our freedoms—*ever!*

Most democratic nations feel that way. That's why it's such a special and wonderful club to belong to. Like any members of a club, democracies don't always agree, but they work very hard to help one another (as "allies") and to solve problems through diplomacy ("talking") rather than fighting.

You probably will not be surprised to know that Afghanistan is an example of a country that is NOT a democracy.

23

Home of the Brave!: They Came to Help— Firefighters, Police, the Military, Civilian Volunteers, and Others

Immediately after the tragic terrorist actions on September 11, 2001, something special happened. It was not surprising—it always seems to happen when a disaster or catastrophe occurs. What was it? People came to the aid of others! Within minutes of the airplane crashes into the World Trade Center's twin towers, New York City firefighters and police swarmed into the flaming buildings. Their goal: rescue as many survivors as possible!

Perhaps if you turned on the television, you heard the sirens? While the sound of screaming firetrucks, police cars, and ambulances can be frightening, they blare the comforting news HELP IS ON THE WAY! As many people escaped down the stairways of the damaged buildings, the brave rescue workers sped UP the stairs, determined to do their job, putting the safety of others first. Unfortunately, many of these rescuers lost their lives while doing their duty. Fortunately, a few were later rescued from the rubble by their fellow firefighters and police officers!

In New York, Washington, D.C., and Pennsylvania, many brave people came to the aid of those in need. This included doctors, nurses, ambulance drivers, and other medical workers. It also included military personnel who went

into action to protect America and its president and citizens from further harm. Also, many civilians jumped right in to do what they could to help. Some donated medical supplies; others prepared food for the rescue workers. Some people donated blood; some collected or gave money for the victims of the disaster.

America is often called "the home of the brave."

List three reasons why you think this is so:

1 _____

2 _____

3 _____

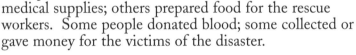

(24)

WE DO NEED ANOTHER HERO!

"Your Say" Essay!

What do you think it takes to be a real-life "hero"?

_____

_____

_____

_____

_____

_____

_____

_____

_____

_____

I Want To Help! : What Kids, Families, and Schools Can Do to Help

After the airplane crashes, building collapses, and other disasters of September 11, 2001 brought on by terrorists, many Americans wondered what they could do to help. Below are things you, your family, or your school might be able to do. Add your own ideas, as well!

YOU!

- Give or collect money (even small amounts help!) for the victims or those who help them
- Write thank-you cards to rescuers; write sympathy notes to those who have suffered losses
- Be especially helpful and thoughtful at home and at school while everyone figures out how to cope with this tragedy

FAMILY

- Say prayers for those who hurt
- Discuss other ways you can help as the days, weeks, and months pass
- Fly the American flag on your house or in your yard

SCHOOL

- Study and learn together what happened, why, and what it may mean in the future for our nation
- Discuss tolerance, understanding, education, and other things that may play a role in helping the world be a better place, less apt to resort to violence
- Organize donation collection, letter-writing campaigns, or other activities that students of all ages can participate in

26

ALL "HELPING" HANDS ON DECK!

Answer the following questions:

Why do I feel so strongly the need to help in a time of crisis?

_____

_____

_____

_____

How does it make me feel to know that even a kid can help?

_____

_____

_____

_____

How would I feel if I were the one being helped?

_____

_____

_____

_____

27

OTHER DAYS THAT WERE DIFFERENT!

September 11, 2001 was a "day that was different" in American life. It was the first time that an act of terrorism of such a large size and caused by non-Americans happened right here in the United States. We know that such major events can change us personally, and even change our nation and our way of life. Even when it seems like there is no good news on such a day, later we can often look back and see how we were able to turn tragedy around to improve our future days.

Here are examples of three other "days that were different" in American history and positive things that resulted from them:

● **April 12, 1861: First shot of the U.S. Civil War fired on Fort Sumter, South Carolina**

After four years of bloody battles with brother fighting brother and many deaths on both sides, America realized that there had to be a better way to solve disagreements than a war between groups of our own people.

● **December 7, 1941: Bombing of Pearl Harbor by Japan**

Following this attack, America joined its allies in World War II to help defeat Germany and its allies, giving freedom back to many nations.

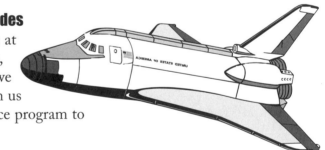

● **January 28, 1986: Space shuttle *Challenger* explodes**

Many students watched this disaster on TV while at their desks in school. Because Christa McAuliffe, the first teacher to travel into space, was aboard, we learned how even teachers might sacrifice to teach us new things. Improvements were made in the space program to help prevent such disasters in the future.

● **April 19, 1995: Alfred P. Murrah Building in Oklahoma City is bombed**

Timothy J. McVeigh, an American citizen, put a bomb in a truck in front of the building and set it off. The explosion destroyed the building and killed 168 people. Oklahoma City National Memorial honors the victims, survivors, rescuers, and all those involved. The victims included 19 children, most of whom were at a day-care center in the building. The field of 168 empty chairs stands as a reminder of each life lost.

Learning From Days That Are Different!

REMEMBER: There will always be days that are "different." Sometimes these days are good! Sometimes they are bad. We must learn from both types of days.

LIST 3
OF YOUR BEST DAYS SO FAR:

_____

_____

_____

LIST 3 OF THE BEST DAYS
YOU THINK WILL COME FOR YOU:

_____

_____

_____

29

Is This the "First War" of the 21st Century?

Following the terrorist attacks on New York City and Washington, D.C. on September 11, 2001, United States President George Bush called this the "first war of the 21st century." Unfortunately, we know that history, including American history, has been blotted with many wars. Some of these wars include:

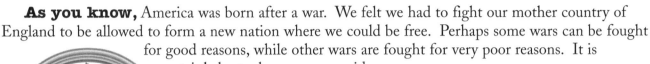

- Revolutionary War ● Civil War ● World War I
- Korean War ● World War II ● Gulf War
- Vietnam (never officially declared as a war)

As you know, America was born after a war. We felt we had to fight our mother country of England to be allowed to form a new nation where we could be free. Perhaps some wars can be fought for good reasons, while other wars are fought for very poor reasons. It is certainly best when we can avoid any war.

War changes over time. Once, soldiers fought face-to-face with little more than sticks and knives. Guns changed war. Nuclear weapons changed war. Computers, airplanes, and satellites in space changed war. Today, we know war continues to change. We see what seem like senseless terrorist attacks all over the world. We have read of deadly chemicals being released in Japanese subway stations. Scary newspaper headlines talk about germ warfare.

If this attack, and America's and the rest of the world's response, does become the "first war" of this century, then it may be fought in old ways and new ways. No one believes we can allow terrorists to have their way. But how we stop them will be what this new "war" will be about.

Answer the following questions:

Can wars be for good reasons? YES   NO   MAYBE   DON'T KNOW

How can we avoid wars? _____

_____

_____

_____

President Bush says Americans are "resolved" to stop terrorism. Circle the word that most nearly means the same thing as *resolved*:   AFRAID   DETERMINED   WISHY-WASHY

30

Enduring Freedom

Americans were surprised on September 11, 2001, when our very own airplanes were used as missiles to attack our buildings and innocent civilians. Surely, we felt, this should not happen in "the land of the free and the home of the brave"? The truth is, terrorist attacks should not happen to anyone.

It is not surprising that America's immediate response was a great, big, loud: "NO!" *No, you can't do that! No, we won't take it! No, you can't get away with this!* Other nations, many of which had citizens die in the attacks, agreed—enough was enough! Once people have freedom, they do not take it lightly, and they will not give it up easily.

We know that this "day that was different" immediately did affect some of our freedoms: airports were closed; the stock market shut down; and many other things happened that, frankly, we are just not used to! As America, and other nations of the world, conduct their war against terrorism, some of our usual freedoms may be affected. Perhaps it will take longer to get through airport security. You may have to show more identification to prove you are you! And international travelers may find it more difficult to come across our borders.

However, these inconveniences are worth the sacrifice if it means we can put an end to terrorism. Everyone, after all, deserves ENDURING FREEDOM!

CIRCLE THE INCONVENIENCES YOU WOULD PUT UP WITH TO HELP PROTECT OUR FREEDOM:

Long lines at airports   Tougher security   More armed guards

Having to show more ID   Being asked questions if someone was suspicious of you

Other: _____

31

What Will America Do Next?

On the morning of September 11, 2001, something happened to America. Out of the clear blue, terrorists hijacked airplanes and used them as missiles to destroy buildings, our peace, and our confidence. In spite of our surprise, shock, and dismay, Americans quickly responded. First we tried to take care of the injured and rescue survivors. Then we spent time respecting and remembering those who died. Next we planned our response to these horrible and unfair attacks. Everyone agreed that it would take a long time to recover from this terrible day.

So, what will America do next? Put an N beside each item you have seen America begin to do now, and an F about things you expect us to do in the future:

___ Clean up the mess

___ Help the injured recover

___ Help those who suffered losses

___ Get businesses going again

___ Repair and rebuild buildings

___ Establish memorials, scholarships, and funds for victims

___ Determine who was guilty for the attacks

___ Punish those who took part in the attacks

___ Improve our security at airports and other places

___ Work with other nations to put an end to terrorism

___ Learn more about why some people would attack America in this way

___ Communicate better why terrorism is wrong and why nations should not allow terrorism

___ Learn more about other countries, peoples, religions, and cultures

Now, add your own suggestions:

_____

_____

_____

_____

RESOLVE VERSUS REVENGE

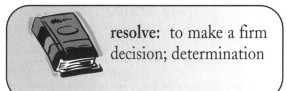

resolve: to make a firm decision; determination

There were many reactions to the attack on America by terrorists on September 11, 2001: shock; sadness; anger. Our immediate reaction was to do what we could to help rescue people. We saw firefighters, police, and others jump right into action, putting the safety of others first. Many rescuers lost their lives trying to help. Others saved many lives, including those of fellow firefighters! Our government was busy trying to be sure that no further terrorist acts occurred.

As things began to settle down, new emotions emerged. We were angry, and naturally so. "Who would do this to us?" we wondered. "And why?" Likewise, we felt very strongly that we had to do something to punish those who had done these bad deeds and to stop them from ever doing such things again.

One emotion we felt was RESOLVE. It is easy to say, "I think I want to do something" or "We probably should do something" about a problem. But Americans, and many others around the world, felt much more strongly than that—they RESOLVED to do something about the worldwide problem of terrorism.

Resolve is different from revenge. If we want "revenge," we just want to "get even," to "get back at them," to punish others, maybe even anyone. Revenge is about making us feel better. Resolve is about being determined to find a solution to a problem.

Because the hijackers of the airplanes used to attack America were Arabs (people from an Arabic-speaking nation), and Muslims (people who practice the religion of Islam), some people wanted to strike back at ALL Arabs and ALL Muslims. This, we know, is not right. It is ok to resolve to bring the people guilty of terrorism, or of helping terrorists hide or escape, to justice.

Put a check in the box to indicate whether an activity represents resolve or revenge:

	Resolve	Revenge
Striking back at anyone and everyone	☐	☐
Arresting people we have evidence may be guilty	☐	☐
Bringing people we have evidence against to trial	☐	☐
Punishing innocent people from the same ethnic group or religion as those who are found guilty	☐	☐

33

©Carole Marsh/Gallopade International/800-536-2GET/www.gallopade.com/Here & Now Series—The Day That Was Different

What Good Can Come From This Experience?

The events of September 11, 2001 were some of the worst experiences of most Americans' lives. Throughout our lives, we may have many experiences we think of as "bad" and later learn that some "good" did come out of them. For example:

Experience	Bad	Good
A drunk driver hits my car	I am am scared, angry, and hurt	I learn that I can recover, that people help me, and that patience and perseverance make me stronger
A fire burns down my house	My family is homeless	I discover that people come to our aid, that we can rebuild, and the fact that we all survived is the most important thing
I lose my job	I am nervous, afraid, and insecure about getting a job as good as the one I had, or getting a job at all	I learn new skills, get a better job, and learn to depend on myself more in my career

Of course, it is difficult for us to imagine how "good" can come out of the "bad" of this tragic day of terrorist attacks. However, we have already seen much good:

•People helping people
•Volunteers donating blood
•Nations joining together in the name of peace

Now, you name three good things:

• _____

• _____

• _____

Here are other good things that I believe can eventually come out of this tragedy:

_____

_____

_____

_____

_____

_____

_____

_____

 34

Tolerance and Your Role as a Student

It is difficult to understand the thinking of the terrorists who attacked America on September 11, 2001. We know that many terrorists believe they are "right" . . . that it is "ok" for them to attack innocent people . . . that they feel Americans are "wrong" and "bad" . . . and that they think the United States "deserves" to be attacked. While it is easy for us to say, "They are crazy!" "They are the ones who are bad and wrong," or, "We should just kill their people right back!"—it is always good to stop and take time to think about what has happened to us.

While nothing can truly explain the actions of terrorists, and we will never agree with them and they may never agree with us, there are many mistakes we can make that do not help matters. Just a few of these include:

• *Blame every person who is like the terrorists.* After the attacks, some innocent Muslims were attacked, even though they are patriotic Americans, who not only had nothing to do with the tragedy, but also had some of their loved ones killed in the attacks.
• *Kill innocent people needlessly, just to "get even."* We need to punish the guilty, not the innocent.
• *Refuse to even think about "those people."* Ignorance is never a good idea, no matter what the subject or the situation.

Perhaps one key to helping put an end to terrorism is to make a more peaceful nation of our own. While we do not like to think of ourselves as "terrorists," we can try to be sure that we are not bullies, that we do not practice intolerance against those who are different from ourselves, and that we do try to understand all people, even if we do not agree with them.

It is often said, "the world is getting smaller and smaller." On the notepad at left, explain what this means and how it is connected to the idea of getting along with people.

 35

THINGS TO DO: IMPROVING YOU

Following the September 11 disaster, you heard adults say many surprising things: "I don't even know where Afghanistan is." "I've never even met a Muslim." "I really don't know much about the terrorist situation today." "I wish I knew more about . . ."

Students may feel this way too. But this is something we know what to do about! Here's how you can be more knowledgeable about historical and current events:

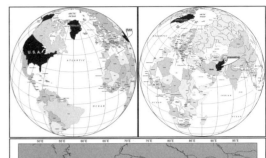

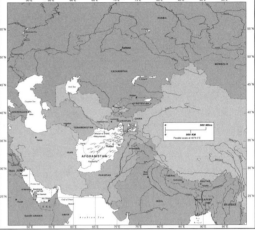

• **Bone up on your geography!**: Look at maps and atlases and locate places mentioned in the news.

• **Visit the school or public library.** Log onto the Internet to learn more about Afghanistan, its people, and its country.

• **Hit the history books!** You are now a witness to history. What other history interests you? Don't forget to talk to elderly people—they have been a witness to some amazing American and world history.

• **Meet a Muslim!** Perhaps someone of this faith can visit your classroom and tell you about their religion.

• **Have discussions.** Many Americans are dismayed when we learn people in other nations judge all Americans by the rock music videos or other limited information they see about us. Do we do the same thing to them? Why do we know so little about one another? How can we change this?

START NOW! KEEP IT UP! NO MATTER WHAT YOUR AGE, YOU ARE A CITIZEN OF THE WORLD AND A PART OF ITS FUTURE!

36

Dear Diary

Each of us is feeling many emotions after hearing that our airplanes were hijacked, our buildings were destroyed, and Americans were killed during the terrorist attacks on September 11, 2001. We learned it was good to cry, to help, to talk with others, to stay close to our family, and to pray. Another way to help cope with your feelings is to write them down. On the diary page below, record any feelings you would like to write down. If you want to continue your diary, make copies of this page before you write on it, or start a notebook diary with this as the first entry.

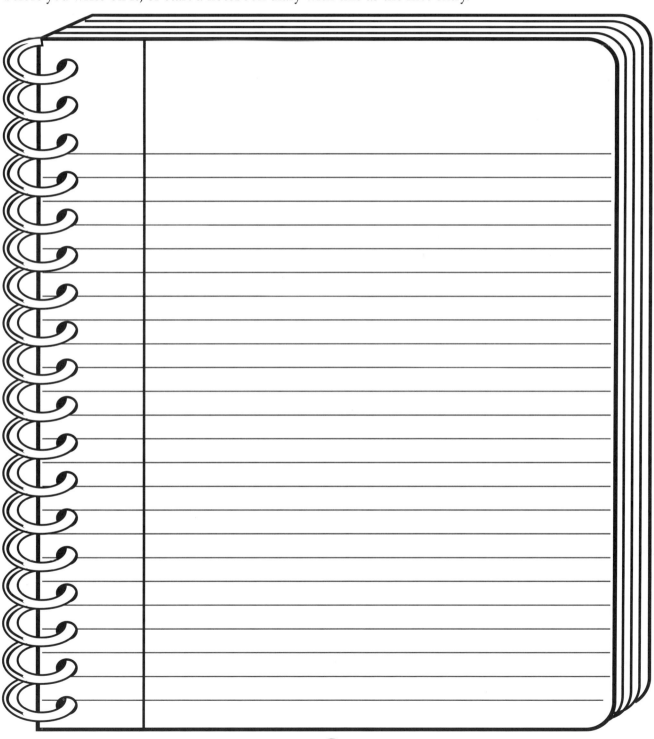

Dear Friend

Communication always helps to cure the blues and blahs that come even long after suffering a tragedy that you cannot understand. This will certainly be true for a long time to come after the sad events that took place on September 11, 2001. Perhaps you have already written a thank you letter to a firefighter or a sympathy note to someone who lost a loved one in the tragedy. You might even have written a letter to the President of the United States! To continue your communication "coping," continue to write letters. Letters are about friendship, sharing, and understanding. Hopefully, someone will write you back! A "dialogue" gets us talking. Talking gets us agreeing. And agreeing gets us getting along with one another. And that's always a good thing!

On the notepad below, write a short letter to a friend, a stranger, your ownself, or anyone anywhere around the world that you care to! It's ok to say what you feel.

You may also write to the author of THE DAY THAT WAS DIFFERENT Activities: Carole Marsh, c/o Gallopade International, 665 Hwy. 74 S., Ste. 600, Peachtree City, GA 30269 USA

38

PRIDE AND PATRIOTISM!

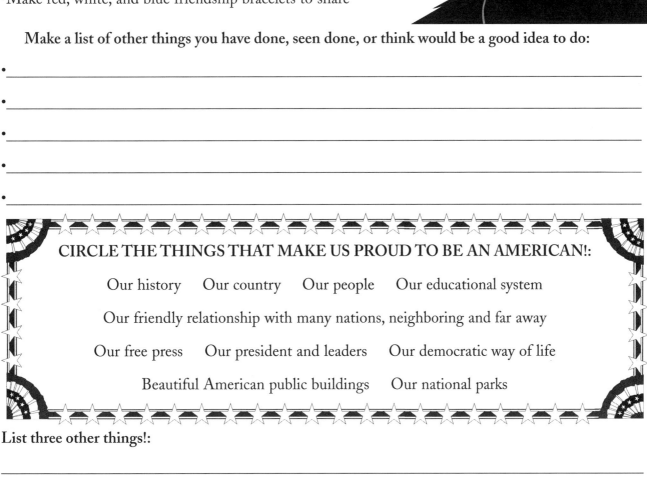

One of the best things that came out of the tragedy of September 11, 2001, now often referred to as Tragic Tuesday, was an immediate increase in the demonstration of American pride and patriotism! (We were always proud to be Americans and very patriotic, but this unfortunate event made us want to show our feelings loud and clear!)

> **pride:** to feel especially good about something
> **patriotism:** to have great pride in your country

Here are a few patriotic things you may have seen or done yourself:
- Display the American flag
- Say the Pledge of Allegiance
- Sing "God Bless America" or other patriotic songs
- Make red, white, and blue ribbons to wear
- Make red, white, and blue friendship bracelets to share

Make a list of other things you have done, seen done, or think would be a good idea to do:

- _____
- _____
- _____
- _____
- _____

CIRCLE THE THINGS THAT MAKE US PROUD TO BE AN AMERICAN!:

Our history   Our country   Our people   Our educational system

Our friendly relationship with many nations, neighboring and far away

Our free press   Our president and leaders   Our democratic way of life

Beautiful American public buildings   Our national parks

List three other things!:

_____

_____

_____

 (39)

Pride and Patriotism, Faith and Hope!

In the years to come, as the war against terrorism around the world takes place, there are many things you can do to help!

I. Have **pride** in your nation. Be proud that you are tolerant of others. Have pride in democracy, freedom of speech and religion, and all the other good things that Americans and other democratic nations enjoy.

II. Be patriotic! Express your **patriotism** in many ways: fly the flag; pick up litter; stay informed; learn the words to those patriotic songs we love to sing!

III. Have **faith**. America has been through tough times before. Our response to those tough times made us who and what we are today. There are many good people around the world working for peace. There are not so many "bad apples" in the bully barrel, after all. As Civil Rights leader Dr. Martin Luther King, Jr. once said, "We shall overcome"—and good will overcome evil.

IV. Hope! Hope is Help+Optimism+Promise+Energy. If you help in any way you can, if you stay optimistic about a positive outcome, if you promise yourself to be part of the solution to problems, and if you act energetically to do all these things, then you can hope for the best outcome possible!

Now, list one way you can have:

Pride:_____

_____

Patriotism:_____

_____

Faith:_____

_____

Hope:_____

_____

 40

Normalsville: When Will the End Be in Sight?

Will things ever be back to normal?, you might wonder. In some ways, things may already feel mostly "back to normal." Some us even felt a little guilty going to school, and playing soccer, and laughing— when we knew so many people were still hurting. Of course, many people reminded us that upsetting our normal, everyday lives was one of the terrorists' goals. So, it seemed like getting back to normal as soon as possible, while not forgetting what happened, was the wisest thing to do.

As a nation, we will never be able to go back to "before" more than 5,000 innocent people were killed in this dastardly attack by terrorists. Just as in the past, no one could "go back" to *before* the assassination of Abraham Lincoln or John F. Kennedy . . . to *before* the Holocaust or Pearl Harbor . . . to *before* Vietnam. Historic events become a part of our lives, and end up molding and shaping our futures.

USS Arizona Memorial, Pearl Harbor

However, life always goes on. This time it goes on with a new awareness that the world is not always a nice place. That bad people can do truly evil things. And that it really is a small world, after all. But we will always be heartened by the heroes we remember. Encouraged by the energy spent to help one another. And dedicated to the world determination that terrorism should end.

Normalsville? You may never find it on a map. But you will always be able to locate it in the smile of a friend, the handshake of a neighbor, or a hug from Mom or Dad.

Go, on—go give it a try, right now!

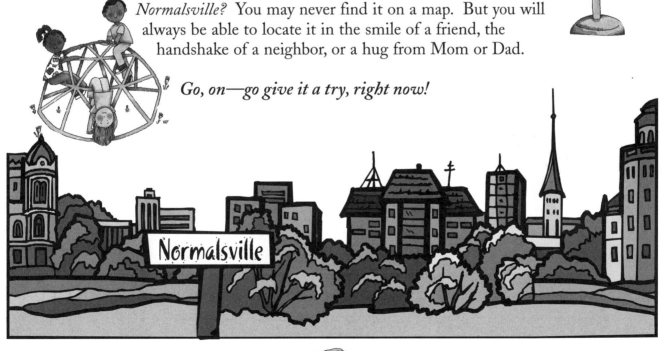

Normalsville

My Questions for Further Discussion

Our minds were filled with questions after the tragic events that unfolded on Tuesday, September 11, 2001. Perhaps some of those questions have been answered. Perhaps many of your questions will never have complete or satisfying answers. But one thing is for sure—it is ok to keep asking them. **Below, list 5 questions that you still would like answers to, or that you think we should continue to discuss as we cope with and recover from this terrible day and its aftermath:**

1 _____

_____

_____

2 _____

_____

_____

3 _____

_____

_____

4 _____

_____

5 _____

_____

_____

42

20 Tips for Parents and Teachers to Help Kids Cope

1. **Be honest with kids.** They know more about what is going on than we think. They are especially tuned in to our reactions. Yes, the event is real. Yes, it is serious. Kids will be more anxious if they think we are afraid to tell them what is happening.

2. **Stick to the facts.** Don't embellish or speculate about what has happened or what will happen. Don't dwell on the scope or the scale of the tragedy.

3. **Be careful not to stereotype religions or nationalities.** Sometimes children generalize a series of negative statements and develop a prejudice.

4. **Keep in mind the age and developmental level of your children.** Younger kids need simplicity and brevity. They need to be reassured that their structure and routine will not change. Older kids will need more information about safety and about what is being done by the authorities. They may also need help sorting reality from fantasy.

5. **Limit and supervise all media exposure.** Most children cannot emotionally process all the sounds and images they could view on television. It is impossible to shelter them from it. The key is to limit and supervise.

6. **Remind kids that there are competent, concerned adults in charge of this situation.** Explain that government leaders, military units, medical personnel, police officers, rescue workers, and others are working around the clock to help people and protect against future crisis situations.

7. **Provide information directly to the students, face to face.** Avoid giving out blanket announcements via the public address system.

8. **Physical proximity is not a bad thing, especially with younger children.** Don't be afraid to read or play quiet games to transition from one activity to the next. Your nurturing presence will comfort them greatly.

9. **Maintain structure and stability with as normal a routine as possible.** Have a plan for the weeks and months ahead of dealing with this crisis. Be a model of calm control.

10. **Allow time for age-appropriate classroom or home discussion and activities.**

11. **Encourage children to talk about their concerns and feelings, whether in general or in response to something specific.**

12. **Never minimize children's anxieties or fears.** A child's fear is justified and is very real to him or her. It's not helpful to say, "There's nothing to be afraid of" or the like.

13. **If children are hesitant to discuss an incident, ask them what they have heard and how it makes them feel.** Let them know that it is okay to feel sad angry, or afraid. Remind them that there are suitable, non-violent ways to express their feelings.

14. **Let kids talk through what they would do in case of a crisis at school or at home.** They need to feel that there are some measures that they can take to be safer, such as fire drills.

15. **Teach age-appropriate ways to call for help, to be safe, and to practice self-defense.** This lesson can be as simple as knowing their last name, address, and phone number as well as how to dial 911.

16. **Monitor use of the Internet.** Yes, the content is disturbing. Kids also need to be aware, though, that personal information such as their name and age can be used by someone who would wish them harm.

17. **Observe the emotional wellbeing of your students.** Some children are especially sensitive. Others may have recently experienced a personal tragedy or had a personal connection to the victims or their families.

18. **Refer children who seem especially distraught to mental health counselors at school.** It will be necessary to inform parents as well.

19. **Find out about school and community resources that are available to help children.**

20. **Children have a strong natural desire to help others.** Provide them an outlet by encouraging them to pray or think hopeful thoughts; helping them make and send get well cards to survivors or letters to the families of victims; or helping them write or make thank you cards and letters for doctors, firefighters, or other professionals who have been helpful through this tragedy.

GLOSSARY
Glossary of Words You May Hear
in the News

Arab: a person from an Arabic-speaking country

bio-warfare: the use of poison chemicals or infectious disease as weapons of war

coalition: a group of people or countries working together to achieve a goal

diplomacy: working toward peace through discussion, cooperation, and compromise

enduring: something that lasts over time

Islam: the religion Muslims practice

jihad: war supposedly fought for a "holy" purpose

muhajideen: fighters in a jihad or "holy war"

Muslim: a person who practices Islam

sanctions: the refusal to trade with a country or do other types of business with them

Taliban: group of men who say that they are the leaders of the nation of Afghanistan; not chosen by the people; not recognized as the official government by other countries

United Nations: a group of countries who work together to solve world problems through peaceful means

Other Resources

BOOKS
Afghanistan
Afghanistan: Fighting for Freedom, by Mir T. Ansary (Macmillan Children Group, 1991)
The Land and People of Afghanistan, by Mary L. Clifford (Harper Collins Children Books, 1989)

Fear and Anxiety
The Safe Zone, by Donna Chaiet and Francine Russell (Morrow Junior Books, 1998)
When Sophie Gets Angry – Really, Really Angry… by Molly Garrett Bang (Scholastic, 1999)

Oklahoma City
One April Morning: Children Remember the Oklahoma City Bombing, by Nancy Lamb (Lothrup, Lee & Shepard, 1996)
A Circle of Love: The Oklahoma City Bombing through the Eyes of Our Children, compiled by Frances Jones, 1997

Pearl Harbor
Pearl Harbor: Opposing Viewpoints, by Deborah Bachrach (Greenhaven, 1989)
Pearl Harbor: America Enters the War, by Terry Dunnahoo (Watts, 1991)

Peace
The Big Book for Peace, by various contributors (Dutton, 1990)
The Peace Commandos: Nonviolent Heroes in the Struggle Against War and Injustice, by Michael Kronenwetter (New Discovery Books, 1994)

Terrorism
United We Stand: America's War Against Terrorism, by Carole Marsh (Gallopade International, 2001)
The War on Terrorism, by J. Messner (Simon & Schuster Trade, 1989)

United Nations
The United Nations Fiftieth Anniversary Book, by Barbara Brenner (Macmillan, 1995)
For Every Child A Better World, by Louise Gikow and Ellen Weiss (Western Publications, 1993)

War
Chemical and Biological Warfare (Dutton 1991)
Battles That Changed the Modern World, by Dale Anderson (Raintree Steck V, 1993)

WEBSITES
CNN has coverage of the story written for the classroom, as well as discussion/activities and lesson plans. Go to http://CNNfyi.com

New York State Department of Education: Crisis Advisory to Schools: http://www.emsc.nysed.gov/crisis/

National Council for the Social Studies provides a forum for discussion of issues regarding the teaching of social studies as it relates to current events such as Tuesday's attack. Go to http://www.ncss.org/resources/moments.html

Helping Children and Adolescents Cope with Violence and Disasters is from the National Institutes of Mental Health: http://www.nimh.nih.gov/publicat/violence.cfm

The National Education Association's Crisis Communication Guide can be found at http://www.nea.org/01crisis.html

Talking to Children and Adolescents After a Disaster is from the American Academy of Child and Adolescent Psychiatry. Go to http://aacap.org/publications/disasterresponse

American Library Association
Books/Videos dealing with the American Tragedy of September 11, 2001: http://www.ala.org/alsc/dealing_with_tragedy_books.html

Federal Emergency Management Agency. Herman the crab teaches how to be prepared for and what causes disasters. http://www.fema.gov/kids/index.htm

MAPS
A Student's Map of Afghanistan: A Country at the Crossroads, by Carole Marsh (Gallopade International, 2001)

The Pledge of Allegiance
...to Color, Say, and Display

1 "I pledge allegiance

2 to the Flag, of the United States of America

3 and to the Republic for which it stands:

4 one nation under God, indivisible,

5 with liberty

6 and justice

7 for all."

My American Flag
...to Color and Display!

©Carole Marsh/Gallopade International/800-536-2GET/www.gallopade.com/Here & Now Series–The Day That Was Different

Author's Biography

Carole Marsh is the creator and author of many educational books for readers 7-17. A native of Marietta, Georgia, the author has been writing children's fiction and non-fiction for more than 20 years. She was named a Communicator of the Year for her corporate communication work in 1979. Marsh is the creator and author of the USA EXPERIENCE, a series of books about America correlated with state learning standards, THE DAY THAT WAS DIFFERENT, a book and reproducible activities package on the events of September 11, 2001, and UNITED WE STAND!, a book and reproducible activities package on the world's war against terrorism. The author has also produced A STUDENT'S MAP OF AFGHANISTAN, and a number of patriotic books and activities in her PATRIOTIC FAVORITES series, including "America the Beautiful!: Lyrics to Color, Sing, and Display," "The Pledge of Allegiance to Color, Say, and Display," "My American Flag to Color and Display Properly," PATRIOTIC FAVORITES COLORING AND ACTIVITY BOOK, and THE YOUNG PATRIOT'S BOOK OF GAMES, PUZZLES, RIDDLES, AND ACTIVITIES. Marsh is the daughter of a World War II veteran. "I believe that we can most help children learn and cope with today's current events through factual, age-appropriate, sensitive, and hopeful materials."

Hey kids! Have your teacher photocopy this page so you can cut out this convenient postcard! Write on it what you thought about this book, and what you might like to see next! Then put a stamp on it and drop it in the mail!

Dear Ms. Carole Marsh:

FROM:

Put Stamp Here

TO:
Carole Marsh
c/o Gallopade International
665 Hwy 74 South, Suite 600
Peachtree City, GA 30269
USA

47

Index